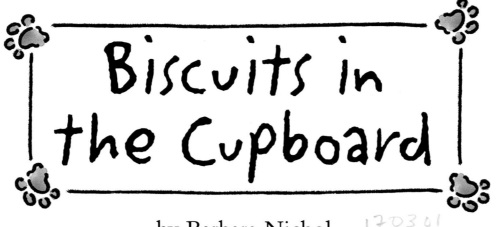

Biscuits in the Cupboard

by Barbara Nichol
illustrated by Philippe Beha

Stoddart Kids

Barbara Nichol thanks Kathryn Cole, Malcolm Lester, Kathy Lowinger, and as ever, David Cole (next of kin). And Sporty.

Book design: Andrew Smith

Stoddart Publishing gratefully acknowledges the support of the Canada Council and the Ontario Arts Council in the development of writing and publishing in Canada.

Published in Canada in 1997 by Stoddart Kids,
a division of Stoddart Publishing Co. Limited
34 Lesmill Road
Toronto, Canada M3B 2T6
Tel (416) 445-3333 FAX (416) 445-5967
e-mail Customer.Service@ccmailgw.genpub.com

Published in the United States in 1998 by Stoddart Kids
85 River Rock Drive, Suite 202
Buffalo, New York 14207
Toll free 1-800-805-1083
e-mail gdsinc@genpub.com

Canadian Cataloguing in Publication Data

Nichol, Barbara (Barbara Susan Lang)
Biscuits in the Cupboard

Poems
ISBN 0-7737-3025-7

1. Dogs – Juvenile poetry. I. Beha, Phillipe.
II. Title.

PS8577.I165B57 1997 jC811'.54 C96-932611-4
PZ7 .N52Bi 1997

Printed and bound in Hong Kong by
Book Art Inc., Toronto.

For John and Elizabeth Nichol
—B.N.

For Fanny
—P.B.

Biscuits in the Cupboard

Biscuits in the Cupboard

Biscuits in the cupboard, way up high.
If I were a bird, oh, I would fly.

If I were a squirrel I'd live in a tree.
If I were a fish I'd swim in the sea.

If I were a clam I'd roll in the tide.
If I were a mouse I'd run off and hide.

Biscuits in the cupboard, way up high.
If I were a bird, oh, I would fly.

First Poems

Dish and Bowl

Dish and Bowl
Dish and bowl
Do I love you?
Heart and soul!

Oh, I'm happy
On the whole,
For I love you
Dish and Bowl.

Rolling

'Round and 'round
Over, under,
Some days sunshine
Some days thunder.

'Round and 'round
Under, over,
Some days dust and
Some days clover.

Cold Nose
(A Summer Song)

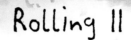

Cold Nose.
Cold Nose.
Blue Skies.
Red Rose.

Sun Shines.
Wind Blows.
True Love.
Cold Nose.

Rolling II

Rolling over
Up to down
Down to up
Around
Around
Turning over
Then about
Shoulder in and
Shoulder out
Muzzle spinning
Tail awhirl
Spinning in
A spinning world.

Sometimes I am happy,
And sometimes I want to cry,
My muzzle's either in the dirt
Or pointed at the sky.

Out for a Walk

Granny Anderson

There goes Granny Anderson.
Each day she comes by here.
Year in, year out, she takes her walk.
Her house is rather near.

Of late I've noticed she's grown old.
She is a little fatter.
Her eyes are dim. Her legs are weak.
She growls if you pat her.

Oh, dear! Perhaps I should explain!
Here is an epilogue:
The lady's name is Betty.
Granny Anderson's the dog!

Heidi and Vida and Cocoa

Heidi and Vida and Cocoa will bark
At whomever they see on the streets.
Please try to remember it isn't their fault.
They have standards that nobody meets.

A Few Small Complaints

Lazy Dog

My grievance is so very small
I'm tempted to forget it.
But when it's you who threw the ball
Why must I go and get it?

The Flea

Wart hog. Bull frog. Kitty cat.
Turtle. Tiger. Sewer rat.
All God's creatures have a right to be.
All God's creatures, except the flea!

No Fleas!

No fleas! If you please!
I've scratched enough today.
I would prefer to spend my time
In any other way.

Oh, fleas! If you please!
Rise up and go away!
For I'd be grateful if you'd find
Another place to play.

Yes, fleas, to leave my weary hide I warmly do invite you.
Nobody likes the kind of guests who feel that they may bite you!

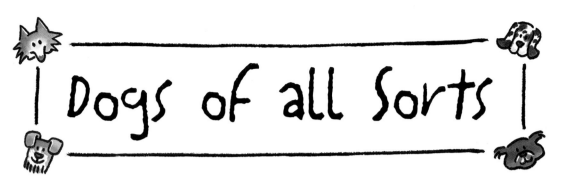

Dogs of all Sorts

A Letter for a Litter

A letter for a litter. Carlotta tends to stray.
A is for the Airedale who was passing by her way.

A letter for a litter. She got away once more.
B is for the Bulldog she had seen somewhere before.

A letter for a litter. Where did Carlotta go?
C is for the Collie I have heard she didn't know.

A letter for a litter. Where can that dog be found?
D is for the Doberman she met down by the pound.

A letter for a litter. Each time another mate.
You'd think the people where she lives would learn to lock the gate!

Great Dane

I would love to appear in this book
But while at a very young age
I grew rather big and by now am too large
For my picture to fit on the page.

Beagle

Other dogs will sit and stay.
Beagles like to run away.

Chihuahua

I'm terribly small, but dreadfully proud.
I'm not one to feel humble or lowly.
Except for one thing: my legs are so short
I must run very fast to go slowly.

Toby is a Crocodile

When you see him in his basket, Toby seems to be asleep.
But though his eyes are closed, our Toby isn't counting sheep.
I have for you the kind of news you won't hear every day—
Not only is he wide awake, he's very far away.
While you might hear outside the distant sound of passing feet,
In Toby's ears there throbs a most exotic jungle beat.

For oftentimes the self inside is not the self that shows.
Oh, Toby is a crocodile, but only Toby knows.

Where you see just a muzzle there are terrible swift jaws.
And he has ghastly talons where you see just fuzzy paws.
Despite the false impression that his furry coat creates,
Toby's covered nose to tail in thick and horny plates.
You might not see the reptile in the basket by the chair,
But that you do not see it, doesn't mean it isn't there.

For oftentimes the self inside is not the self that shows.
Oh, Toby is a crocodile, but only Toby knows.

His teeth are sharp as razors and his eyes are sharp as teeth.
A sunny surface has this dog, with darker depths beneath.
The fish dive to the riverbed, the birds are mute with fear.
Not any beast, however cruel, would ever dare go near.
And so, while Toby seems to doze unmoving on the floor,
He slips into the water and he glides away from shore.

For oftentimes the self inside is not the self that shows.
Oh, Toby is a crocodile, but only Toby knows.

The Legend of Chicken Bones

The Legend of Chicken Bones

Cracks and Crackles, Tears and Groans.
Do you hear him? Chicken Bones!

There is an old and chilling tale, a story dogs will tell
Long after dark on summer nights to weave an eerie spell.

"And what," you ask, "can be the tale that keeps them up so late?"
It is the dreadful story of a bad dog's awful fate.

A foul and filthy beast he was, a mean and mangy cur,
With glinting eyes and foaming jaws and greasy, reeking fur.

But it was not these things which brought him to his nasty end,
(Though certainly his stinking did most probably offend.)

He was, as well, an outlaw and he liked to break the rules.
(Law abiding dogs, he thought, were simpletons and fools.)

Scrapes and Scratches, Shrieks and Moans.
Right behind you! Chicken Bones!

His hideout, so they say, was in a town called Spider Lake.
And it was there he broke a law that dogs must never break.

The law is one that every thinking animal condones.
And that's the law forbidding them from eating chicken bones.

Now why this dog he ate those bones is never to be known.
He died as he had lived, and that was utterly alone.

In any case he crunched them up between his greedy jaws.
And so he met his end that night with chicken bones the cause.

Snaps and Crunches, Cries and Moans.
Look around! It's Chicken Bones!

He died by eating chicken bones.That's how he got his name.
And on that night he won a sad and dreadful sort of fame.

For though he's now a skeleton, he does not have a grave.
He walks the earth instead to frighten dogs who don't behave.

And if the many stories of this skeleton are true,
He breaks the rules and scares a lot of very good dogs, too.

(You see, for many years he has had neither sleep nor food
And rumor has it this has not done wonders for his mood.)

And finally they say his bones do scrape and crunch and crack.
In every step there are the noises of his fatal snack.

Creaks and Crumples, Thuds and Groans.
Save my soul! It's Chicken Bones!

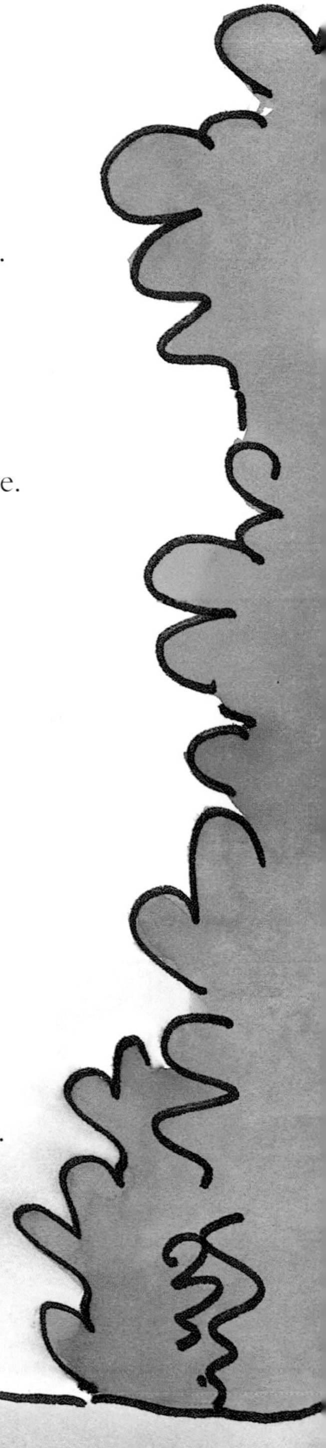

And when the story's over, not a dog will make a sound.
Their breath is very shallow, and their eyes are very round.

And huddled close, their hearts will pound at any sound they hear.
For any sound could be a sign that Chicken Bones is near.

A Verse to Whisper

In the rustle of the treetops
In the creaking of the floor
In the snapping of a twig
And in a knock upon the door
In a scuttle in the pantry
In a foot upon the walk
In the ringing of the phone
And in the ticking of a clock
In the roar of distant traffic
In the scraping of a chair
In any sound can be a clue
That Chicken Bones is there!

Rhymes and a Riddle

A Riddle

Every morning at this time
You see me going into town.
From where you are I seem to be
A big white dog with ears of brown.

Every evening without fail
You see another dog go back.
This dog, it seems, looks just like me
Except this dog has ears of black.

Here's the riddle you must solve.
And so that clues you will not lack,
Now think! A brown-eared dog goes by.
Why does a black-eared dog come back?

Another hint:

My father was a brown-eared dog,
A black-eared dog my mother.
You see me mornings from one side
And evenings from another.

A Foolish Old Fellow

A foolish old fellow from Dover
Named all of his many dogs Rover.
Each time he called one
A stampede was begun,
And his Rovers, of course, knocked him over.

A Winter Limerick

Three pups: Biggins, Baggins and Boggins,
All winter have lumps on their noggins.
The lumps are because
Having not hands, but paws,
They cannot hold on tight to toboggans.

The Tail

The nose, up front, begins the hound.
Beneath, four paws upon the ground.
Above, the middle, without fail.
And at the end—at last—the tail!

R.I.P.
Here lies Madelaine
O'Flannery O'Conner.
Once she was a Basset Hound,
But now she is a goner.

In the Park

John and George

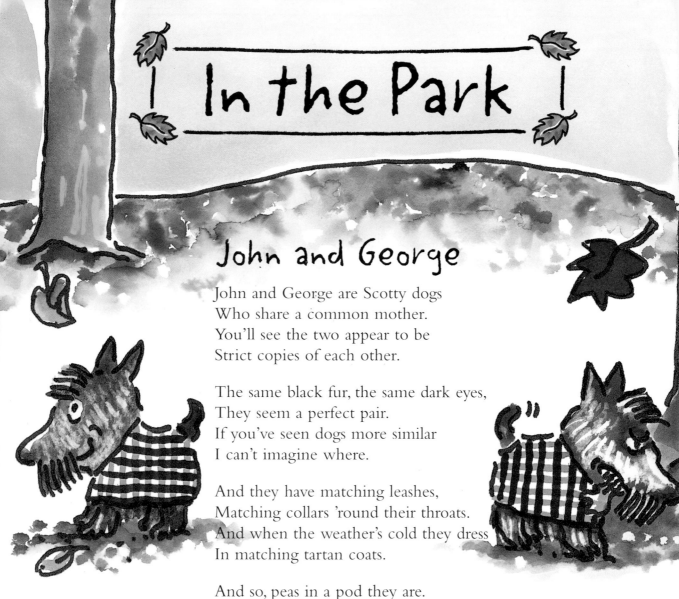

John and George are Scotty dogs
Who share a common mother.
You'll see the two appear to be
Strict copies of each other.

The same black fur, the same dark eyes,
They seem a perfect pair.
If you've seen dogs more similar
I can't imagine where.

And they have matching leashes,
Matching collars 'round their throats.
And when the weather's cold they dress
In matching tartan coats.

And so, peas in a pod they are.
That's how these two appear.
But there's one little difference, which
You'll find if you come near.

John and George, they seem the same;
Same weights, and widths, and heights.
But bend down close and you will find
The one named George. . .HE BITES!!!

Little Nonnie

Some dogs are very tiny. Little Nonnie's one of these.
Each day he makes his way across the park and through the trees.
He doesn't stop to pass the time or look to either side.
It seems that being small is not a barrier to pride.

Autumn

Frost upon the morning grass,
Berries on the trees.
When I am old
I will remember
Mornings such as these.

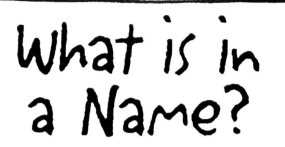

What is in a Name?

Toughie

Toughie run! Toughie hide!
Where not a soul can trace you.
For when the bad dogs hear your name
They're surely going to chase you!

Anonymous

I call my dog Anonymous.
(This poem is eponymous.)

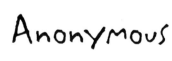

What is in a Name?

Killer is a friendly dog.
Rusty isn't red.
If Sporty had his way he'd spend
From dawn to dusk in bed.

Rover never leaves the yard.
Waggins has no tail.
Tiny is so big she eats
Her dinner from a pail.

Fluffy's coat is very thin.
Racer's rather slow.
Lucky's had a bee sting now
Two summers in a row.

Happy tends to howl a lot.
Marauder's very tame.
And Mister is a lady dog.
So what is in a name?

The Tale of Canadian Jim

The Tale of Canadian Jim

You might know the name of Canadian Jim.
He's a dog of some fame and renown.
But there was a time I remember quite well
When he came to reside in our town.

Canadian Jim had a head full of dreams.
He had always a plan in his pocket.
And so, when one morning he passed a high fence,
He made up his mind he would walk it.

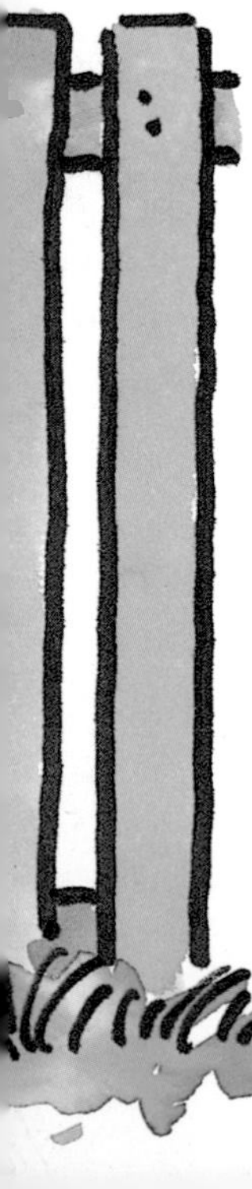

He climbed on the fence and at first he fell off.
At the start he was tippy and slow.
But he practiced and soon an idea took shape;
He decided to put on a show!

He learned how to walk down the fence, did our Jim.
He was limber, and nimble, and spry.
He perfected a twirl and a leap for the end
And invited the crowds to drop by.

When the crowd was in place, he performed on the fence
All dressed up in his very best collar.
So fine was the show that the group soon agreed
When he asked if they might pay a dollar.

The crowd came each day with great pleasure to watch
Our friend Jim, who had mastered the fence.
Because they were regulars, Jim said all right
When they asked to pay just fifty cents.

Now, Jim grew more expert. He added a jig.
And the show became longer (not shorter).
But Jim so enjoyed it, the crowd rightly guessed
He would still do his show for a quarter.

A picture of grace he became before long.
A master of movement and mime.
He made it seem easy. (Of course, it was not.)
And they soon offered Jim just a dime.

They promised to pay him a dime from then on,
But townsfolk are terribly fickle.
And if you know townsfolk, (and if you know rhymes),
You'll know they soon paid him a nickel.

By now he was famous, Canadian Jim!
His audience numbered so many.
"Reward in itself!" as the crowd did explain
When they said they would pay him a penny.

Jim heard their new offer from up on that fence
And answered with something quite clever.
"I *will* take your penny, and here's what you'll see.
For a penny I'll leave here forever!"

Out the Back Door

Out the Back Door

Kitten on the fence post,
Squirrel up the tree,
Mice behind the wood pile,
All awaiting me.

Inside Out

I'm very aware that it's lucky for me
That to change your mind isn't a sin.
For when I am inside I want to go out.
When I'm outside I want to come in.

Backyard Behavior

I'll make my case against the cat
In very simple words.
It's true I dig up flower beds.
At least I don't eat birds!

A Bright Day

A bright day. A shiny day.
As shiny as a dollar.
That's the day I'll go away
Without my leash and collar.

Paw Prints

Paw prints on the pathway.
Where does life go?
I was a puppy
A long time ago.

Paw prints on the pathway.
How can it be
Paw prints will be one day
All that's left of me?

Off to Sea

Dog Fish

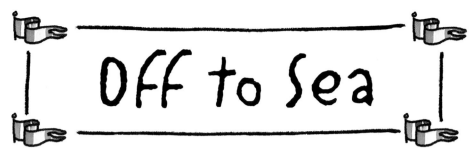

Dog fish. Dog fish.
Come up and visit me!
Oh, I have heard that there are puppies
Living in the sea.

A Sea Song

One paw for shaking and two paws for begging.
There was a brave dog who set sail in a boat.
Three paws for limping and four paws for running.
This dog couldn't swim, but he knew how to float.

Sailor's Song

I am a dog
Set out to sea,
Alone on the blue
Just the wind and me.
A dog for adventure
Bound to roam,
I'll be never
Sailing home.

In the Night

In the Night

Jumping up,
Jumping down,
On and off the bed.
While others sleep
I like to take
Some exercise instead.

Bat

Bat above me in the dark:
I can't fly, but you can't bark.

Thunder

There's crashing in the summer sky.
It's Chicken Bones! He's passing by.

Memento

Memento

I'll leave my scent
Upon this tree
Someday
Someone
Please think of me.